Dr. Jekyll and Mr. Hyde

by Robert Louis Stevenson

Abridged and adapted by T. Ernesto Bethancourt

Illustrated by Rick Nederlof

A PACEMAKER CLASSIC

FEARON / JANUS / QUERCUS
Belmont, California

Simon & Schuster Education Group

Other Pacemaker Classics

The Adventures of Huckleberry Finn
The Adventures of Tom Sawyer
A Christmas Carol
Crime and Punishment
The Deerslayer
Ethan Frome
Frankenstein
Great Expectations
Jane Eyre
The Jungle Book
The Last of the Mohicans
Moby Dick
The Moonstone
The Red Badge of Courage
Robinson Crusoe
The Scarlet Letter
A Tale of Two Cities
The Three Musketeers
The Time Machine
Treasure Island
20,000 Leagues Under the Sea
Two Years Before the Mast
Wuthering Heights

ISBN 0–8224–9255–5
Library of Congress Catalog Card Number: 84–60925

Printed in the United States of America.

10 9 8 7 6
MA

Contents

Introduction

Almost a hundred years ago Robert Louis Stevenson wrote *Dr. Jekyll and Mr. Hyde.* It was popular then, as it is today. Plays and movies have been made of the story. Even TV has used the idea. Who has not seen it in one form or another? The picture of a good man who becomes evil when he takes a drug has been painted many times. Still, it stays in the minds of all who have seen it.

In the 1800s, we knew little about drugs. We knew even less about what drugs can do to the mind. How could Robert Louis Stevenson have seen so far ahead? It seems that the idea for *Dr. Jekyll and Mr. Hyde* came to Stevenson in a dream. He wrote it down in a few weeks, even though he was very sick with tuberculosis at the time. His wife read it and thought it was the worst story he had ever written. Because she was so upset, Stevenson burned his only copy.

Not long after that he changed his mind. He decided to write it again. According to his wife, it took him all of six days to do it. It was accepted by a publisher in London. But it became more popular in the United States than in England.

To this day the story is a lesson to everyone. It is a lesson about drugs and how they can change anyone who uses them.

1 Story of the Door

Mr. Utterson, the lawyer, was a man who didn't smile often. Yet he had many good friends who liked him. He was a strict man, but he had a good nature. Really, he was more strict with himself than with other people. For he believed in the saying, "Live and let live."

One day Utterson and his cousin Richard Enfield were taking a walk through London. It was sometime in the late 1800s. They came upon a bright, cheerful street, full of shops. All the houses and shops had been newly painted, but one. It was the one house that didn't face the street. All you could see was the back. The house had two floors, but no windows could be seen. In fact, you could only make out an unpainted wall and an old door that was very dirty.

"Have you ever noticed that door?" Enfield asked Mr. Utterson. "Something very strange once happened to me, right near this door."

"And what was that?" asked Mr. Utterson.

"Well, it was this way," Enfield began. "I was coming home from some place at the end of the world, one cold winter morning, about three o'clock. No one was on the street. It was dark, and

I would have felt better if there had been a policeman around.

"Suddenly," Enfield went on, "from where I stood, I saw two people. They were both headed toward the corner, from either side. One was a little girl in shabby clothes. The other was a small man, well dressed. He was walking very fast. When they both came to the corner, they ran right into each other. I couldn't believe what happened then. The little man knocked the girl down and walked right over her!"

"By mistake?" asked Utterson.

"I think he wanted to do it," Enfield said. "He didn't even stop. He left her crying in the street. It was an ugly thing to do. It was even uglier to see. He was walking away, leaving the poor girl hurt and crying.

"I ran after him and grabbed him by the coat. I took him back to where some people had gathered around the little girl. These people were her family. They had sent her sister to get a doctor.

"Once we were near the streetlight," Enfield continued, "I got a good look at the man who ran the girl down. He was short and ugly. But there was more to it than that. There was something about him that could almost make you sick, just looking at him. It was as if something *evil* lived inside him.

"Just then the doctor arrived," Enfield added. "He looked at the hurt girl and said she would be all right. The doctor seemed to be one of those men who stay cool, no matter what kind of terrible sight he sees. He took one look at the ugly man I held by the coat. I could see by the doctor's face that he felt the same as I did about this evil little man: He wanted to kill him.

"The little girl's family were going crazy," Enfield went on. "They started to shout at the evil man. I think that if the doctor and I had not been there, they would have tried to kill him. I knew in my heart that if they had attacked him, neither the doctor nor I would have done much.

"Then the doctor and I got together," Enfield continued. "We told the evil little man that unless he made things right for the girl and her family, we would tell the world about the awful thing he had done. You'd think this would have made the man feel bad, but it didn't. He was cool as ice. We could all see that he didn't care about the girl at all. He sneered when he said, 'All right. Tell me how much money you want.'"

"What a cold person," Utterson said.

"I'm with you on that," Enfield agreed. "Then the man did the strangest thing. He took out a key, went right to that door over there, and went inside. He came out in a few minutes with a check for a lot of money. But it wasn't signed by him. The name on the check was that of a well liked, very good man. A man all of London knows. I told him I didn't think a man so good could have a friend so evil. I also said that the check might be a fake. He sneered again and said, 'Don't worry. I will stay with you until the banks open.'"

"Which is what he did," Enfield went on. "I saw to it that the girl's family got the money."

"Did you notice the address of the man who wrote the check?" Utterson asked. "Was it the same as this house with the dirty door?"

"I did," Enfield answered. "It was different from this place. Something or other square."

"There is one other thing," Mr. Utterson said. "What was the name of this evil little man? It's very important that I know."

"You talk as if you know something about this," Enfield said.

"Yes, I do," Utterson replied. "So think well about what you have told me. Is there anything you have left out? I must know."

"You could have told me you knew," Enfield said, a little angry. "But yes. I have seen the man again. He still has the key to the house over there. I saw him use it, not a week ago."

"Is there anything you want to add about the way he looked?" Utterson asked.

"Only that he is so evil that he makes you think there is something wrong with the whole form of his body. Yet I can't tell you just what he looks like, even though I can still see his face—that evil, evil face."

"And his name?" Utterson asked.

"Hyde," Enfield said, "Mr. Edward Hyde!"

2 Search for Mr. Hyde

That night Mr. Utterson came home feeling very low. He ate his dinner without tasting it. Most Sundays, when his meal was over, he would sit in his chair by the fire and read a good book. He would read until he heard the church bells at midnight, then go to bed. But this Sunday, as soon as his meal was over, he took a candle and went to his office in the house. There, he opened his safe and, from its most secret part, took out a paper. It was Dr. Jekyll's will.

The will was only a copy. When Dr. Jekyll had made it, Mr. Utterson had said he would have no part of it. He had said this once he knew what was in it. The will stated that in case Dr. Jekyll died, everything he had would go to his "good friend, Mr. Edward Hyde." The will went on to say that in case Dr. Jekyll, for any reason, "should be missing for more than three months," Mr. Hyde would step right into Dr. Jekyll's shoes. All Mr. Hyde had to do was to give some money to the people who worked for Dr. Jekyll.

Mr. Utterson had never liked this will. He hardly ever looked at it. Up until now, he was angry at this Mr. Hyde, though he had never seen him. But now that Enfield had told him how evil Hyde was, Utterson was even more angry. Why would a good man like Dr. Jekyll leave all he had to such a wicked man?

"At first I thought Jekyll was going mad," Mr. Utterson said to himself. "Now I think it's worse. I think this Mr. Hyde has something on Dr. Jekyll."

Saying this, Mr. Utterson put out his candle. He put on his hat and coat and went to Cavendish Street, a very rich part of town. It was on Cavendish Street that the great Dr. Lanyon lived. "If anyone knows about this, it will be Lanyon," Mr. Utterson muttered to himself. "After all, Lanyon is one of Jekyll's closest friends."

Dr. Lanyon's butler brought Mr. Utterson right to Dr. Lanyon. The doctor was having dinner. He was sitting alone at a table, drinking wine.

Dr. Lanyon was a big man, a bit fat, with a healthy red face. He talked loudly and liked to make jokes. He was always great fun to be with. His hair was white, even though he wasn't very old. As soon as Lanyon saw Mr. Utterson, he smiled happily and rose from the table. The two men shook hands warmly. The doctor and Mr. Utterson were very old friends.

"I suppose, Lanyon," the lawyer said, "you and I must be the two oldest friends of Henry Jekyll's."

"I wish we were both younger," Dr. Lanyon said, making a small joke. "But I suppose you are right. But what of it? I see very little of Jekyll now."

"Really?" said Utterson. "I thought you were such good friends."

"We were," Lanyon agreed. "But almost ten years ago, Henry Jekyll's medical ideas got too wild for me. He began to go wrong—wrong in his mind. I still like him, for old times' sake. But I don't see him at all. His strange ideas would drive any friend away."

The doctor seemed to be very upset. But this very thing made Mr. Utterson feel better. "They have had a fight about some medical ideas," Utterson said to himself. "It's nothing worse than that." He gave his friend a few minutes to pull himself together. Then he asked:

"Tell me, did you ever come across a friend of Jekyll's—a man named Hyde?"

"Hyde?" Lanyon asked. "No, I never heard of him. He must be a new friend of Jekyll's."

And that was all Utterson got from his talk with Dr. Lanyon. The lawyer went home and went to bed. But he still couldn't sleep. By six o'clock in the morning, he was still awake. What was this all about? Up until now, Mr. Hyde had been only a name in Dr. Jekyll's will. As Utterson tried to sleep, pictures came into his mind: He saw the evil little man who was Mr. Hyde. He saw him on the dark street, as he walked over the little girl. He heard her screams, as Mr. Hyde went his way, not caring what he had done.

In his mind he also saw his friend, the good Dr. Jekyll, asleep in his own bed, smiling at his dreams. Suddenly, the evil Mr. Hyde would be there, at Dr. Jekyll's side. Hyde would wake up the doctor to make him do whatever evil things Hyde wanted him to do. But in Mr. Utterson's mind, Mr. Hyde had no face. Even Enfield had not been able to say just what Hyde looked like. Mr. Utterson began to get an idea.

He had to see this Mr. Hyde—to really set eyes on him. He felt if he saw Hyde, he could clear things up. At least, it would be a face worth seeing—the face of a man who was without the smallest bit of good in him.

From that time on, Mr. Utterson began to stay near the door where Hyde had run down the little girl. He stood where it had happened. Night and day, before and after work, Mr. Utterson would be there . . . looking . . . waiting . . . hoping to see the evil Mr. Hyde. Utterson thought to himself: "If he is Mr. Hyde, then I will be Mr. Seek!"

Then, at last, it happened. It was a dark, cold night. There was no wind to blow out the street-lights. It was ten o'clock, and no one was on the street. You could hear every small sound, even if it were very far away.

All of a sudden, Utterson heard someone walking toward him. It was a light step such as a rat would make in the dark. Utterson hid in a nearby doorway. The steps came closer. Then they got louder. Mr. Utterson looked out from where he was hiding, and saw a man.

The man was small and thin. He was dressed in plain clothing. Even from far away, there was something about this man that made Utterson dislike him. The small man went right to the door—the very door where Enfield had seen him. Then he took out a key, as if he were returning to his home.

Mr. Utterson stepped out of the dark and grabbed him. "Mr. Hyde, I think?" he said.

Mr. Hyde drew back and hissed, almost like a snake. But in a second he got himself together. He didn't look the lawyer in the face, but he said cooly:

"That is my name. What do you want?"

"I see you are going in," the lawyer said. "I am an old friend of Dr. Jekyll's—Mr. Utterson, of Gaunt Street—you must have heard my name. Now that we have met, I thought you might let me come in with you."

"You will not find Dr. Jekyll here," Hyde said. "He is not at home." And then suddenly, but still without looking up, he asked, "How did you know me?"

"I will tell you if you do one thing for me," Utterson said.

"And what is that?" asked Hyde.

"Will you let me see your face?" asked the lawyer.

Mr. Hyde waited for a second. Then, as if he were making up his mind, he did as the lawyer asked. The two men looked hard at each other for a few seconds. They didn't say a word.

"Now I will know you if I see you again," Utterson said. "It may be useful."

"Yes," Mr. Hyde said. "It's just as well we have met. And you should know where I live, too." He gave Utterson a street number in a part of town called Soho.

"This is bad," Utterson said to himself. "Can Hyde be giving me his street number because he has read Dr. Jekyll's will?" But he didn't tell Hyde what he was thinking.

"And now," asked Mr. Hyde, "how did you know me?"

"Someone told me about you," Utterson said.

"Who?"

"A friend of both of ours," the lawyer said.

"What friend is that?"

"Dr. Jekyll," Utterson said.

"He never told you!" Mr. Hyde said, suddenly red in the face and angry. "You are lying! I did not think you would lie to me!"

"Easy now," Utterson said. "That is no way to talk—to call me a liar."

Mr. Hyde gave an evil laugh. Before Utterson could do anything, Hyde opened the door and went inside. He closed the door in the lawyer's face. Utterson stood there with a troubled look on his face. Then he began to walk away, slowly. Every few steps, he stopped. He put his hand to his head, like a man with a great weight on his mind. He had to think hard. What was this about? What was there about this evil little man that made him dislike him so very much?

It was true that Hyde's body seemed strangely formed. He was short and seemed shy and pushy at the same time. But these things were not enough to make Mr. Utterson hate the man. "There must be something else," he said to himself. "There *is* something more, if I could only find a name for it. He seems to be less than a man. He seems hardly human! Maybe it is what is *inside* Mr. Hyde that makes him seem so evil. Oh, my poor friend, Jekyll! If I have ever seen the face of the devil himself, it is the face of your new friend, Edward Hyde!"

Mr. Utterson walked around the corner from where he had met Mr. Hyde. This street did not have shops. It had only very well-kept houses. Well-to-do people lived on this street. One house had lights in its windows, even though it was late. Utterson walked up to this house and knocked on the door. A butler answered. Mr. Utterson knew the man. His name was Poole. He worked for Dr. Henry Jekyll. And this was the fancy house in which Dr. Jekyll lived.

"Is Dr. Jekyll at home, Poole?" asked the lawyer.

"I will see, Mr. Utterson," said Poole, as he let the lawyer inside. He led him to a sitting room. There was a bright fire, and it was a warm change from the cold street. It made Utterson feel that seeing Mr. Hyde had been a bad dream. He waited a few minutes while Poole went to see if Dr. Jekyll were home. This was fine for Utterson. He had always liked this room in Jekyll's house. In a few minutes Poole came back. He told the lawyer that Dr. Jekyll had gone out.

"I saw Mr. Hyde go in by the back door," the lawyer said. "Is that all right, Poole, when Dr. Jekyll is out?"

"Oh yes," Poole said. "Mr. Hyde has a key."

"Dr. Jekyll must like Mr. Hyde very much to let him have a key."

"Yes, he does," Poole answered. "And all of us who work here must do what Mr. Hyde tells us to do. Dr. Jekyll has said so."

"I do not think I ever met Mr. Hyde when I had dinner here?" asked Utterson.

"Oh, dear, no, sir," Poole said. "He never *eats* here. We see very little of him on this side of the house. He comes and goes by that back door."

"Well, good night, Poole," Utterson said.

"Good night, Mr. Utterson."

On his way home, the lawyer said to himself, "Poor Henry Jekyll. I think he is in deep waters! He was wild when he was young, but that was a long time ago. Maybe this Hyde has found out something that Jekyll did years ago. That is his hold on him. It *must* be. I have known Dr. Jekyll a long time. He is a good man. But wait! If this Hyde is as evil as he seems to be, there is still hope. Maybe I can break his hold on Jekyll. God help poor Jekyll if Hyde ever finds out about the will he has drawn up. I think if Hyde knew of it, he would even kill poor Jekyll to get his money!"

14

3 Dr. Jekyll Gives a Dinner Party

Two weeks later, Dr. Jekyll gave one of his famous dinner parties. Many well-known people were there. Of course, Utterson was also a guest.

Utterson waited until all the others had gone. He often did this at the doctor's dinner parties. The doctor liked to talk with Utterson when everyone had left.

"I've been wanting to speak with you, Jekyll," Mr. Utterson said. "You know that will of yours?"

If you had looked closely at Dr. Jekyll's face for just a moment, you would have seen a strange, troubled look. Then he smiled happily and said to his lawyer:

"My poor Utterson. You have such bad luck to be my lawyer. I never saw a man so upset as you were about my will. You acted the way Lanyon did about my medical ideas. Oh, I know Lanyon is a good fellow. But he has a closed mind. Any new ideas, and he goes wild. I feel that he let me down, behaving the way he did."

"You know I never liked it," Utterson said. He didn't want Dr. Jekyll to start talking of other things.

"My will?" asked the doctor. "Yes, I know you never liked it. You have told me so many times."

"Well, I tell you so again," Utterson said. "What is more, I have learned a few things about young Mr. Hyde."

Dr. Jekyll's face grew pale, right to his lips. A dark look came into his eyes. "I don't care to hear more," he said. "I thought we were going to drop it. Say no more about my will."

"What I have heard about Hyde is bad. I can't bring myself to say it," Utterson said.

"What you have heard can't change things," Jekyll replied. "You can't know the spot I am in. It's very strange. And talking about it isn't going to change it."

Utterson put his hand on Jekyll's arm. He smiled at his friend and said: "Jekyll, you know me. You know I would never tell anyone. Tell me the truth. Maybe I can get you out of this spot you are in."

Jekyll smiled sadly. "Utterson, this is good of you . . . very good of you. I cannot find the words to thank you. I would trust you more than any man in the world—even myself. But don't be afraid for me. It isn't as bad as you think. And if it makes you feel better, know this: The moment I choose, I can be rid of Mr. Hyde. I give you my hand on that. And I thank you again and again. I will add just

one little word. This talk of ours is a private matter. I ask you to let it stay secret."

Utterson sat looking into the fire, saying nothing. After a time, he got up and said, "All right, Jekyll."

"Well, then," said Dr. Jekyll with a smile, "I hope we have said the last of it. There is one more thing I would like you to know. I have a great interest in poor Hyde. I know you have seen him. He told me so. I'm afraid he wasn't very nice to you. But I really do have a great interest in that young man. And if something should happen to me, Utterson, I ask you to bear with him."

"Oh, really!" Utterson cried.

"If you knew the whole story," Jekyll said, "you would understand Hyde and see that he gets what is coming to him."

"All right," Utterson said, "but I know I will never like the man."

"I don't ask that," Jekyll said, laying his hand on the lawyer's arm. "I only ask you to help him for my sake, when I am no longer here."

"Well, then," said Utterson sadly, "I promise to do as you ask."

4 The Carew Murder Case

A year later, in the month of October, all of London was upset by a murder. The man killed had been very important. The story went this way:

A maid, who worked in a house near the river, went to bed about eleven o'clock. The moon was very bright that night, and she couldn't fall asleep right away. She got up and sat by her window. She looked at the street below her. Later she told of what she saw.

She had seen a tall, white-haired gentleman come down the street. Coming at him, from the other way, was a little man. He walked with a strange light step. She didn't look at him too much. The white-haired older man, so good-looking, held her eye. The two men came together right under her window.

The moon lit the face of the tall man. The woman said to herself: "I never saw such a nice face—so warm and kind." He stopped to say something to the little man. The woman thought that the tall man was asking for help. He had probably lost his way. Then she saw the other man.

She knew him right away as a certain Mr. Hyde. She had seen him before. Hyde had come to the house of the man she worked for. She had only seen him for a few minutes back then, but she had known she hated him. If you had asked her why, she could not have told you. There was just something evil about the man—something she could not name.

Hyde had a heavy walking stick in his hand. As he talked to the tall man, he played with the stick. Suddenly, with no warning, Hyde got very angry. He shook the stick under the tall man's nose. He began to shout at him. The older man took a step back, a hurt look on his face. Then, Hyde began acting like a wild man. He began hitting the man with his stick again and again. The poor man fell down. This did not stop Hyde. Again, and still again, he hit the man with his heavy walking stick. Hyde began to jump up and down upon him. When the woman heard the poor man's bones break, she passed out.

It was two o'clock in the morning when she came to. She called the police. The killer had run away by then. The poor old man's body still lay in the street. The police found part of the heavy walking stick near the body. Hyde had hit the man so hard that he had broken the heavy stick! The police thought that Hyde had taken the other part of the stick with him, when he ran away. The killer had not stolen anything from the fallen man. The police went through his pockets. Nothing was missing. Among other things, they found

a letter to Mr. Utterson. The poor man never got to mail it.

The police came to Utterson's house with the letter. He was still in bed at the time. They showed him the letter and told him what had happened.

"I shall say nothing until I have seen the body," Utterson said.

Utterson ate his breakfast and dressed as fast as he could. Then he went with the police to where they had taken the body. As soon as he saw it, the lawyer said, "Yes, I know this man. I am sorry to say that this is Sir Danvers Carew."

"Good God, sir," cried the policeman, "can it really be?" Then a sly look came over the policeman's face. "This case will make a lot of noise around London," he said. "The policeman who finds the killer will be a very important man. Maybe you can help us find the murderer, Mr. Utterson."

Then the policeman told Utterson what the woman at the window had seen and heard. He showed the lawyer the broken piece of walking stick. Utterson's face grew pale when he heard the name of Mr. Hyde. When the policeman showed him the broken stick, Utterson didn't want to believe it. Even though it was broken, he recognized the stick. Utterson had given it to a friend as a gift many years ago. The friend he had given it to was Dr. Henry Jekyll!

But Mr. Utterson said nothing about the stick. He only asked the policeman, "Is this Mr. Hyde a small man?"

"Very small and very evil looking is what the woman called him," the policeman said.

Mr. Utterson shook his head sadly. "If you will come with me," he told the policeman, "I think I can take you to his house."

By this time, it was about nine in the morning. A heavy fog had settled over London. It was very hard to see. The cab in which the men were riding had to move very slowly.

The fog was so heavy that it seemed to Utterson that the city of London was on fire. Thick smoke seemed to cover everything. Or maybe, he thought, Hyde's crime was so bad that London was trying to hide itself. He and the policeman came to the part of London called Soho. In the fog, Soho seemed like a bad dream. Buildings appeared to be falling down. No one seemed to care. Some of the buildings had not seen a coat of paint in many years.

The cab came to Mr. Hyde's house. The fog lifted a bit. Utterson could see the rest of the street. It was dark and dirty. There was a gloomy bar, a dirty-looking restaurant, and a few stores. Children dressed in rags sat in doorways. Strange people came and went. Then the fog came back. All Utterson could see was the house where Edward Hyde lived. This was the home of the man who would someday get all of Jekyll's money. They got out of the cab. The policeman knocked at the door.

A white-haired woman, with an evil face, opened the door. She acted nicely enough. But Utterson felt she was doing just that: acting. Yes, she explained, these were Mr. Hyde's rooms. But he was not at home. He had come home very late last night. Then he had gone out again right away. But this was not strange for Mr. Hyde. He often came and went at strange times. In fact, until today, she had not seen him for almost two months.

"Very well, then," said Mr. Utterson, "we wish to see his rooms."

The woman said she could not let them in because Mr. Hyde was away. Then Utterson said, "I had better tell you who this person is. This is Inspector Newcomen of Scotland Yard."

The woman smiled an evil smile. "Ah, he is in trouble, then! What has he done?" She seemed happy that Mr. Hyde was probably in trouble with the police.

Mr. Utterson and the inspector looked at each other. "It seems no one likes Mr. Hyde very much," the policeman said. To the woman, he said, "And now, my good woman, just let me and this gentleman have a look at Mr. Hyde's rooms."

They looked all through the house. The woman who worked for Hyde used one room. Hyde used only two for himself. The rest of the rooms were empty. But the two rooms Hyde used were filled with things that showed very good taste. The closet was filled with good wine. The picture on the wall was very costly. These items seemed out of place for a run-down building in Soho. Utterson thought that the picture was probably a gift from poor Dr. Jekyll.

At this moment, however, it looked as if a storm had struck the rooms. Clothes were lying on the floor. Their pockets were turned inside out. The inspector found the other part of the heavy walking stick. It was behind a door. This pleased him very much. In the fireplace they found a partly burned checkbook. They could still read the name of the bank where the checkbook had come from. Utterson and the inspector left Hyde's house. They went right to that bank.

They found out that Hyde had a lot of money in there. This made the policeman even happier. "You can be sure," he told Utterson, "I have him in my hand. He must have lost his head after the murder. Or he never would have left the stick or burned the checkbook. The checkbook was a big mistake. Why, money's life to the man. All we have to do is wait at the bank. He will try to get his money. Then we'll get him for sure. Now, what does he look like? I want to have pictures drawn of him."

This was not as easy as the inspector thought. Hyde had been seen by very few people. There were no photographs of him at all. When people were asked to describe him, they had the same trouble as that of Enfield and Utterson. All they could say was that he was young, small, and had an air of evil about him. The police kept looking for Hyde.

5 Story of the Letter

It was late in the day when Mr. Utterson found his way to Dr. Henry Jekyll's door. Poole let him in right away. He led Utterson through the house and into a garden. Then they went across a yard to a run-down building out in back. This was Dr. Jekyll's laboratory. Jekyll had bought the house from the family of a doctor who had died. Years ago, the building had been used for cutting up dead bodies, to study them. But Jekyll was a different kind of doctor. He had made the building into a laboratory.

It was the first time that Utterson had ever seen this part of Jekyll's house. Looking at the dark building that had no windows made him feel uneasy. Poole opened the door. He led Utterson through a big room. This was where bodies had been cut up. Utterson imagined how this room had looked years ago. He could see the old doctor showing his students things about the bodies.

Now the room was not used. It was dirty and full of dust. There were tables covered with strange bottles. Pieces of broken boxes lay all about. At the end of the room were some stairs. Poole led Mr. Utterson up the stairs to a red door. They went inside. This was the secret laboratory of Dr. Henry Jekyll.

It was a large room, filled with all kinds of strange things. There were bottles of bad-smelling chemicals. There was glass, bent into strange forms. A flame burned under a big round glass bottle on one table.

There was a large standing mirror and also a heavy chair and desk near the fireplace. In this chair, looking very sick, sat Dr. Henry Jekyll. He seemed as if he were trying to get warm. He sat close to the fire. He didn't get up when Utterson came in. They shook hands. Utterson noticed that the doctor's hand was cold.

"And now," Utterson said, as soon as Poole had left, "I suppose you have heard the news?"

The doctor's body shook. He nodded his head. "It's all over town," he said. "I heard the news-boys. They were crying it in the streets. I could even hear them in my dining room."

"One thing, first," Utterson said. "Carew was my friend. I worked for him, as well. You are my friend, too, but you are still alive. Tell me. You haven't been crazy enough to hide this killer Hyde, have you?"

"Utterson," the doctor said, "I swear to God I will never set eyes on him again. I am done with him in this world. It is all at an end. He does not even want my help. You do not know him as I do. He is safe—very safe. Mark my words, he will never be heard of again."

With a frown on his face, the lawyer listened to what Jekyll had to say. He didn't like the way the doctor was acting. "You seem pretty sure of what you say," Utterson told Jekyll. "For your own sake, I hope you are right. Because if the police get hold of Hyde, I cannot keep your name out of it, you know."

"Oh, I am right," Dr. Jekyll said. "I am very sure he is gone for good. I can't tell you how I know this. But believe me, my friend. Hyde is gone for all time.

"But there is something else I want to talk about," Jekyll went on. "You must tell me what to do about it. I got a letter today. I don't know if I should show it to the police. I'll put it in your hands, Utterson. If you want to give it to the police, then I'll go along with what you do."

"Are you afraid this letter will bring the police down on Mr. Hyde?" asked Utterson.

"No, I don't care what happens to Hyde," Dr. Jekyll said. "I am done with him, as I told you. I was thinking of my own good name."

Utterson sat and thought a while. He was surprised at Jekyll's selfishness. He was now sure that Jekyll wanted to get rid of Hyde.

"Very well," he said, "let me see the letter."

The letter was written in a strange handwriting that sloped backward. At the bottom it was signed "Edward Hyde." The letter said that Hyde was sorry for all the trouble he had caused Dr. Jekyll. He felt bad because Jekyll had been good to him, and he had caused Jekyll a great deal of trouble. He said that Jekyll need not worry about him. He had a plan to get away from the police. He was sure he would be all right. Utterson finished reading the letter. He felt better. Maybe he had seen the last of Mr. Hyde, after all.

"Where is the envelope to the letter?" Utterson asked.

"I burned it," Dr. Jekyll answered, "before I knew what I was doing. But the envelope won't help you find Hyde. It didn't come in the mail. It was handed in."

"Well then," Utterson asked, "shall I keep this, and sleep on it?"

"I will go along with anything you want," the doctor said. "I don't really trust myself anymore."

"All right," Utterson said, "I will think about what to do with this letter. But there is one more thing I would like to know. It's about your will. It was Hyde who told you what to put in it, wasn't it? And that part about your being missing for three months—that too?"

The doctor's face got pale. He said nothing. He only nodded his head. "That's what I thought,"

Utterson said. "He was going to kill you, Jekyll. You have had a close call, my friend."

"I have had more than that," Jekyll said. "I have had a lesson—oh, God, Utterson, what a lesson I have had!" And saying this, he covered his face with his hands for a moment. Utterson left Jekyll like that, sitting in the chair.

On his way out, Utterson stopped to talk with Poole. "By the way," he said to Poole, "there was a letter that came by hand today. The person who brought it, what did he look like?"

"I am sure you are wrong about a letter being handed in, sir," Poole said. "All that came today was by mail. If anyone came with a letter, I would have seen him."

Suddenly, Utterson was afraid for Jekyll again. True, the letter could have been pushed under the laboratory door. Poole would not have seen it then. But what if the letter had been written inside the laboratory? Had Jekyll lied about not having seen Mr. Hyde? If he had lied, maybe Utterson would not give the letter to the police.

As the lawyer walked along, he heard the boys selling papers. They shouted the news of Sir Danvers Carew. "One of my friends is dead. Another friend's good name is in trouble," he said to himself. "What will I do about this letter? If I give it to the police, they will want to talk with Jekyll. If they do, the whole ugly story will come out. Henry Jekyll talks with me when he is in trouble. Most of my friends do, too. But who can *I* turn to?"

He went home and sat by the fire. He sent for Mr. Guest, who worked for him at his law office. Mr. Guest came to Utterson's house. In a little while, both men were sitting by the fire, sharing a bottle of fine wine.

Outside the house, the fog still covered the city of London. Looking out his window, Utterson saw the lamps on the street. He could hardly make them out. But inside, in this room, it was warm and cheerful. Utterson looked at his clerk Mr. Guest. He and this man had shared many secrets. Could he perhaps talk with Guest? Guest had been to Dr. Jekyll's house before. Utterson had sent him there. Because of the will, Guest knew a little bit about Edward Hyde. Should Utterson show Guest the letter? He knew Guest would tell no one. And Guest knew a great deal about handwriting. Maybe if Utterson showed him the letter, Guest could help Utterson make up his mind. The lawyer said to Guest:

"This is a sad thing about Sir Danvers."

"Yes, sir," Guest said. "Everyone is talking about it. The killer, of course, was crazy."

"I'd like to know what you think about that, Guest," the lawyer said. "I have a letter here in his own handwriting. I will let you see it, but you must keep it a secret. I don't know what to do about this letter. But look at it yourself. Here it is: a murderer's handwriting."

Guest's eyes grew very bright. He sat down and looked at the letter. He read it again and again. Then he said, "No, sir. This man is not crazy. But it is a very strange handwriting."

"Written by a strange man," Utterson said. Just then, Utterson's servant came in with a note.

"Is that from Dr. Jekyll, sir?" Guest asked. "I thought I knew the handwriting. Is it something secret, Mr. Utterson?"

"Jekyll asks me to have dinner with him. That's all," Utterson said. "Why? Do you want to see it?"

"Only for a moment. I thank you, sir," Guest said. Then he put the two pieces of paper side by side. He looked at both of them carefully. Then he handed them back to Utterson. "Thank you, sir," Guest said. "It's a very interesting handwriting."

For a time, Utterson said nothing. Then he asked, "Why did you look at them that way, Guest?"

"Well, sir," Guest answered, "the two handwritings are very much alike.

"Strange," Utterson said.

"Yes, it is," Guest replied.

"I wouldn't speak of this note," Utterson said.

"No, sir," said Guest. "I understand."

That night, as soon as he was alone, Utterson put the note in his safe. It would stay there. He thought, "Why would Henry Jekyll write a letter for a killer?" And his blood ran cold.

6 The Death of Dr. Lanyon

Time ran on. A great deal of money was offered in reward for finding the killer of Sir Danvers Carew. But the police were not able to find Mr. Hyde. He was gone. It was as if he had never lived at all. Stories came out about the evil things Hyde had done. No one could say a good word about him. But no one could find him, either. From the time he had left the house in Soho, he had simply vanished.

As time went on, Mr. Utterson's fears for Dr. Jekyll seemed to disappear. He began to act more like himself. The death of Sir Danvers was more than paid for, Utterson felt, by the disappearance of Edward Hyde.

And with Hyde gone, a new life began for Dr. Jekyll. He started to go out again and to see more of his old friends. In the past he had always given to good causes. This, he still did. Now he also became well known for going to church. This was something he hadn't done much before. He was busy. He got out in the fresh air a lot. His face seemed to open and brighten, as if the good inside him were beginning to show on the outside. For two months, Dr. Jekyll was a happy man.

On January 8th Dr. Jekyll gave one of his dinner parties. Dr. Lanyon was there. It was as though they had never had a fight. Utterson, Lanyon, and Jekyll were together once more.

But then, on the 12th and the 14th Utterson found the door to Dr. Jekyll's house closed to him. "The doctor cannot leave the house," Poole said, "and he will see no one." On the 15th Utterson tried again. He heard the same words from Poole. Because Utterson had been used to seeing Dr. Jekyll almost every day, he began to fear for Dr. Jekyll. He went to see Dr. Lanyon.

Dr. Lanyon's butler took him straight to the doctor. When Utterson saw Lanyon, he couldn't believe the change that had taken place in the way the doctor looked. Lanyon's red face was now pale. He had lost a lot of weight and a great deal of hair. He looked much older. What made Utterson feel even more afraid was the look in Dr. Lanyon's eyes. It was a look of fear—a great fear that had no name.

"Maybe he is afraid he will die soon," Utterson said to himself. "But he is a doctor. He knows that death is part of life. Everyone dies. He must know that he hasn't long to live. And he can't take it." Utterson said what was on his mind to Dr. Lanyon. The sick man told him he was right.

"I have had a bad blow," he said, "and I don't think I will ever get over it. It will only be a few weeks before I will die. Well, life has been good to me. I like it. Yes, sir, I used to like it. I sometimes think, if we knew all there were to life, we would be more glad to leave it—to get away."

"Jekyll is sick, too," Utterson said. "Have you seen him?"

But Lanyon's face changed then. He held up a weak hand and said in a loud voice: "I am quite done with that person. I wish to say or hear no more of Dr. Jekyll. And I beg you not to talk about him. I think of him as dead."

"Oh, my," said Mr. Utterson. He said no more for a time. "Can't I do anything?" he asked. "We are three very old friends, Lanyon. We won't live long enough to make other friends."

"Nothing can be done," Lanyon said. "Ask Jekyll himself."

"He will not see me," said the lawyer.

"I am not surprised at that," Lanyon replied. "Some day, Utterson, after I am dead, maybe you will come to learn the right and wrong of all this. I cannot tell you now. And if you can sit and talk with me about other things, for God's sake, stay and do so. But if you cannot stop talking about Dr. Jekyll, then, in God's name, go, for I cannot bear it."

As soon as he got home, Utterson sat down and wrote to Jekyll. He said he was hurt that Jekyll would not see him. He asked what had gone wrong between Jekyll and Lanyon. The next day he got a long letter from Jekyll. Jekyll's words were sometimes sad. At other times they were strange. But one thing was certain: he and Lanyon were no longer friends. Nothing could ever fix that.

"I do not blame our old friend," Jekyll wrote, "but he is right. We must never meet again. From now on, I am going to live a different life. I will live alone from all other men. If you find my door closed to you, don't think it is because I don't like you. I still do. You must let me go my own dark way. I have done something terrible. Now I must pay. If what I have done is awful, so is the price I have to pay for having done it. I did not know what I was doing at first. Now that price is too high. I can't bear to think about it. The best thing you can do is to leave me alone."

Utterson could not believe what Jekyll had said in the letter. Wasn't Jekyll his old self again? Hyde was gone. Everything was going so well. Had Lanyon been right? Was Jekyll going crazy? Or was there something still worse—something Utterson did not know?

A week later Dr. Lanyon took to his bed. Less than two weeks after that, he was dead. A short time after Lanyon had died, Utterson went into his study. He locked the door. He lit a candle and put before him an envelope. On the envelope, in Dr. Lanyon's handwriting, were the words: "This is for the eyes of **G. J. Utterson Alone**. And in case he dies before me, this letter is *to be burned.*"

"Oh, this is sad," Utterson said to himself. "I have lost one of my two best friends. Will this letter cost me the other one?" Then he put his fear to one side and opened the letter. There was still another envelope inside. On the envelope were the words: "Not to be opened until after the death of Dr. Henry Jekyll, or in case he is missing for a long time."

Utterson could not believe his eyes. Here it was again—this "missing" matter. It was like Jekyll's will, all over again. But the will had been written because of the evil Hyde. Now to read the same thing from Lanyon, what could it mean? Utterson wanted to open the letter. He wanted to see what it said. But Mr. Utterson had been a good friend to Lanyon when he was alive. He would also be a good friend now that he was dead. He put the letter away and did not open it. He did not feel good about doing this. But he felt that a friend was always a friend. And a promise was always a promise.

But the letter stayed on his mind. It even changed the way he felt about Dr. Jekyll. He no longer wanted to see him that often. He still liked Jekyll, but in his mind, he was afraid. He was afraid of what he might find out about him. It was far more easy to stay outside Jekyll's house and to talk to Poole. Poole did not have much good news for Utterson. Dr. Jekyll was getting worse. Now he would not come out of his laboratory. From time to time, he would even sleep there. He did not read. It seemed there was something very heavy on his mind. After a while Utterson got tired of hearing the same things from Poole. After that, he didn't go to Dr. Jekyll's house much anymore.

7 A Face at the Window

That Sunday Utterson was taking a walk with his cousin Enfield. They passed the same street where Enfield had first seen Mr. Hyde. When they came to the door, they both stopped and looked at it.

"Well," Enfield said, "that story is at an end, at least. We will never see Mr. Hyde again."

"I hope not," said Utterson. "Did I ever tell you that I once saw him? And I felt the same way you did about him."

"To see the man is to hate him," Enfield said. "By the way, what a fool you must have thought I was. I didn't know this door was the back way to Dr. Jekyll's house. It was because of you that I found it out."

"So you found it out, did you?" said Utterson. "But now that you know, let us step into the back-yard and look at the windows. To tell you the truth, I feel bad about poor Jekyll. I feel he needs a friend, but he won't see anyone."

The yard was cool and even a little wet. But overhead the sky was still bright. The sun was just going down. This side of the building had three windows. One of them was halfway open.

Sitting close to the window, looking out, was Dr. Jekyll. He looked sad.

"Jekyll!" Utterson cried, "I hope you are feeling better."

"I am feeling very low," Jekyll called back sadly, "very low. It will not last long, thank God."

"You stay inside too much," said the lawyer. "You should be out more, as we are. This is my cousin—Mr. Enfield—Dr. Jekyll. Come on, get your hat and coat. Come take a walk with us."

"You are very good," Jekyll said sadly, "I'd like to very much. But no, no, no, no, it is quite impossible, I am afraid. But, Utterson, I am very glad to see you! This is really a great pleasure. I would ask you and Enfield to come in, but the place is really not fit for company."

"Well, then," the lawyer said, "the best thing we can do is to stay where we are and talk with you."

"Fine with me," Jekyll said. "I was going to ask if that was all right with you." He smiled as he said this. Utterson began to think that maybe Jekyll was coming around.

But no sooner had Jekyll said those words when an awful look came over his face. It was a look of a man full of fear—a look of a man who has given up all hope. It made Utterson's blood run cold to see Jekyll's face. Just then, Jekyll closed the window and went away from it.

Enfield and Utterson looked at each other. They did not say a word. They left the backyard of Jekyll's house. That look on the doctor's face had been awful. To talk about it would have made things worse. They went on with their walk. Still, they did not talk. It was not until they came to a busy street, full of lively people, that Utterson could say a word.

Both men looked at each other. They knew what was on their minds. "God help us all," said Mr. Utterson, "God help us all!" Enfield didn't say anything. He just nodded his head. They went on with their walk. Neither man said another word.

8 The Last Night

Mr. Utterson was sitting by the fire one night. He was surprised that Poole had come to see him.

"Poole," he cried, "what brings you here?" Then he took another look at the man. "What's wrong?" Utterson asked. "Is the doctor ill?"

"Mr. Utterson," said the man, "there is something wrong."

"Take a seat, and here is a glass of wine for you," said the lawyer. "Now take your time, and tell me what you want."

"You know how the doctor is, sir," said Poole, "and how he keeps to himself. Well, he's shut up in his laboratory, and I don't like it, sir. I wish I may die if I like it. Mr. Utterson, sir, I'm afraid."

"Now, my good man," said the lawyer, "say what you mean. What are you afraid of?"

"I've been afraid for about a week," said Poole, "I can't take it anymore."

The way Poole looked showed he was telling the truth. He could not look the lawyer in the face. He did not drink his glass of wine. He just sat there, looking at the floor. "I can't take it anymore," he said again.

"Come on, Poole," said the lawyer, "I can see there is something wrong. But I can't help if you don't tell me what's going on."

"I think there's been a crime," said Poole.

"A crime!" cried the lawyer. "What kind of crime? What do you mean?"

"I'm afraid to say, sir," Poole said, "but will you come along with me and see for yourself?"

Utterson's only answer was to get his hat and coat. He saw right away that this made Poole feel better.

Outside, it was a wild, cold March night. There was a little light from the moon, but the wind kept blowing clouds across it. The wind blew hard and cold. Poole and Utterson did not talk much on the way. It was as if the wind were a broom that had swept the people off the streets. It was lonely on the street. The lawyer would have been glad to see a friendly face. It seemed there was something evil in the air—something that kept all the people in their homes.

When they got to Dr. Jekyll's house, the wind was blowing dust all over the yard. The thin trees in the garden were shaking. Poole, who had walked ahead of Utterson, stopped and wiped his wet face. Utterson thought it was not the cold that made Poole sweat. It was fear. His face was pale, and his voice sounded strange when he said:

"Well, sir, here we are. I pray to God that there is nothing wrong."

Poole took out a key and opened the door to the house. Inside, it was bright and warm. There was a fire in the fireplace. All the people who worked for Dr. Jekyll were standing near it. As soon as the cook saw Utterson, she began to cry. She called out: "Thank God! It's Mr. Utterson!" She ran to him and put her arms around him.

"What is this?" Mr. Utterson asked, a little angry. "Why are you all here? Have you no work to do?"

"They are all afraid," Poole told the lawyer. One of the women began to cry out loud.

"Be quiet!" Poole shouted at her. "How can we do anything with all this noise and crying?" One of the servants was standing near the crying woman. Poole looked at the boy and said: "You, boy! Bring me a candle. Now that Mr. Utterson is here, we will get to the bottom of this right away!" Poole took a lit candle from the boy. He led Utterson into the backyard and garden. He held his hand close to the candle, against the wind.

Once they got inside the dirty building in back, Poole said to Utterson, in a soft voice. "Now sir, try to keep still. I want you to hear what is going on inside. But I don't want anyone to know you are here. And, sir, if he asks you to go inside, don't go!"

Utterson didn't say anything. He just nodded his head and followed Poole. They went through the outer room and up the stairs to Dr. Jekyll's laboratory.

Even though Utterson could see that he was afraid, Poole went to the head of the stairs. "Dr. Jekyll!" Poole called. "Mr. Utterson is here. He wants to see you!"

A voice came from inside: "Tell him I cannot see anyone."

"Thank you, sir," said Poole. He came back down the stairs to where Utterson waited. Then the two men went back to the big house. Once they were inside, Poole led the lawyer into the kitchen. He set down the candle and looked the lawyer right in the eye. "Sir," he asked, "was that Dr. Jekyll's voice?"

"It seems much changed," said Utterson.

"Changed? Well, yes, I think so," said Poole. "I have worked in this house for Dr. Jekyll for twenty years. Could anyone fool me about his voice? No, sir. Somebody has killed him! It was eight days ago when I last heard Dr. Jekyll's real voice. He cried out for God to help him. After that, I have heard this *other* voice. But *who* is it? *Why* does he stay there? Oh, this is awful, Mr. Utterson. It cries out for an answer!"

"This is a very strange story, Poole. This is a wild tale," Utterson said. "If, as you think, Dr. Jekyll is . . . well . . . dead, why would the killer stay? It doesn't seem right."

"Well, Mr. Utterson, think about this," Poole said. "All this last week, that *thing* has been in Dr. Jekyll's laboratory. He cries out day and night for some drug. In the past, if Dr. Jekyll wanted something, he wrote a note. He left it on the top of the stairs. That is what *it* has been doing, too. I have gone to every big drugstore in London this week. Each time I bring back the drug he wants, I leave it on the stairs. I do the same with his meals. Each time I leave the drug, I get another note. The notes always say that the drug is not pure—not good enough. Each note tells me to try another store. He wants that drug very badly, sir. And I wish I knew what for!"

"Do you have any of these notes?" Utterson asked.

Poole felt in his pocket and came up with a crushed piece of paper. The lawyer got close to the candle to see it better. The note said: "This last drug you sent me was not pure. A few years ago, I got a large amount of this same drug from you. If you have any of it left, I need it now. This new drug is no good. I don't care how much it costs. Get it for me! For God's sake, get me some of the old drug!"

"This is a strange note," Utterson said. "And why have you opened it? You shouldn't read other people's mail."

"The man at the drugstore was so mad, he threw it in my face," Poole said.

"But this *is* Dr. Jekyll's handwriting, isn't it?" the lawyer asked.

"I don't care about that," Poole said, very upset. "Because I *saw* him!"

"Saw him? What do you mean? Saw *who*?"

"It was this way," Poole said. "I was coming from the house. I was bringing him a meal. When

I got to the laboratory stairs, I saw him there. He was looking to see if I had brought the new drug, I guess. He looked up and gave a cry, like an animal. Then he ran inside. He shut the laboratory door. Sir, if that were Dr. Jekyll, why did he have a mask on his face, and why did he run from me? I only saw him for a second. But what I saw made the hair on my head stand up!" Poole put his hands over his face.

"Easy now, Poole, easy," said Utterson. "You may have things all wrong. I will tell you what I think. I think that Dr. Jekyll is very sick. It has changed the way he looks. It has bent him over and made him look different. I'm sure he was wearing some kind of mask to hide the changes in his face. That must be why his voice sounded different. It's very important for him to have this drug, so he can get well again."

Poole looked Utterson in the eye. He stood up tall. "Mr. Utterson," Poole said, "Dr. Jekyll is a tall man. What I saw was a small, bent *thing*! Don't you think I know the doctor after twenty years? Don't you think I know how high his head comes to at the laboratory door? I have seen him each morning for many, many years. No, sir, that *thing* in the mask was not Dr. Henry Jekyll. I think the doctor has been murdered!"

"If you keep up this way, Poole," the lawyer said, "then I will have to make sure. But I don't want to hurt Dr. Jekyll. This note, in his own handwriting, seems to show he is still alive. What do you want me to do? Break down the door?"

"Ah, Mr. Utterson," Poole cried, "that's talking!"

"Then we will do it together, Poole," Utterson said. "I will see to it. If the doctor is still alive, you won't get into trouble because of it."

"Good," Poole said. "There's an ax downstairs. And I can get a poker for you, if you want." The man went and got both tools. When the lawyer was holding the heavy poker in his hand, he looked at Poole and said:

"You know, Poole, this is a very grave thing we are about to do."

"Oh, yes, sir," said Poole.

"Then I think we should say what is really on our minds, don't you?"

"Yes, sir, I do," said Poole.

"Then tell me, Poole. This *thing* in the mask . . . did you know him?"

"Well, sir, he went back into the laboratory very quickly. I can't be too sure. But if you mean, was it Mr. Hyde?—why, yes, I think it was! You see, he was about the same size. And he moved in that same light way. And who else could get in by the back door of the laboratory, but him? He has a key. But that's not all. I don't know, Mr. Utterson, if you ever met Mr. Hyde?"

"Yes," the lawyer said. "I spoke with him once."

"Then you must know that there is something strange about the man—something that gives you a turn. I don't know just how to say it, sir. But there is something about him that makes your bones feel cold all over."

"I know what you mean" the lawyer said. "I felt it, too."

"Well, that's what I mean, sir. When I saw this *thing* in a mask run into the laboratory, it made me feel cold. Now, I never had much schooling, Mr. Utterson. I'm not a smart man. But I give you my word it was Mr. Hyde!"

"I knew it, I knew it!" cried Utterson. "That's what I was afraid you would say. Evil was sure to come of Jekyll's interest in Hyde. And now it *has* come! Poole, I believe you. I think poor Henry Jekyll is dead. And even though I don't know why, I think his killer is behind that laboratory door. Let's get him! Call Bradshaw."

Bradshaw was a man who worked for the doctor. He took care of the horses and drove the doctor around town. He was a very big, strong man. Poole went and got him. When Bradshaw, Poole, and the lawyer were together, Utterson said:

"I know you are upset about all this, Bradshaw. But pull yourself together. Poole and I are going to break down this door. We can do that, all right. We are big enough. When we break down the door, the man inside may try to get away through the back door. I want you to take one of Dr. Jekyll's servants and wait outside. Take a couple of heavy sticks with you. And don't be afraid to use them. I'll give you ten minutes before we start breaking down the door!" Once Bradshaw left, Utterson said to Poole, "Let's get going."

He took the poker under his arm and led the way through the garden. The clouds covered the moon. It was very dark. The wind blew at the candle. It made the shadows jump. Inside the backyard, you could hear the sounds of London. But these sounds seemed far away. It was still in the yard. Listening closely, you could hear the sound of someone walking inside the laboratory.

"So he will walk all day," Poole said, "and the better part of the night, too. There's only a break when some of the new drugs come from the stores. But if I had the blood of two men on my hands, I'd be walking up and down that way, too. Listen to him! There is death in every step he takes. But listen closer, sir. Does that sound like the way Dr. Jekyll walks?"

The lawyer listened. Poole was right. Jekyll's walk was slower and heavier. Even when this *thing* in the room walked slowly, it was a light step. "Is it like this all the time?" Utterson asked.

Poole nodded. "Once," he said, "I heard it crying!"

"Crying? What do you mean?" Utterson asked. Suddenly he felt cold all over.

"Crying like a woman—or a lost child," Poole said. "It could break your heart to hear it. When I heard it, I could have cried, too."

Now the ten minutes were up. Poole picked up his ax. The two men set the candle in a place where it would not blow out. Then they got to the top of the stairs. They could hear the steps inside, going back and forth . . . back and forth. Just before Poole was ready to use his ax, Utterson called out:

"Jekyll, I must see you! If you don't open this door, we will have to break it down!"

"Utterson," said the voice, "In God's name . . . don't do it!"

"That's not Jekyll's voice," cried Utterson, "It's Hyde's! Down with the door, Poole!"

Poole used the ax. The blow seemed to shake the building. He hit the door again. It began to break open. A scream, more like an animal's than a person's, came from the laboratory. Up went the ax again, and then down. But the door was made of heavy wood. It took five blows to break it down. When it fell, the two men ran into the room. Then suddenly, they stopped. They looked around.

They thought they'd see a dead body and things all about. They were wrong. The room was very neat. There was a fire going. Some papers, also neatly placed, were on a desk. There were even tea things laid out! Except for the jars and bottles of drugs, the room could be any room in a nice part of London.

In the middle of all this was a body on the floor. It was all bent. It was shaking like a tree in the wind. The two men turned it over on its back. They saw the face of Edward Hyde! He was dressed in clothes that were too big for him. They looked as if they were really Dr. Jekyll's. And even though the body was still moving, it was easy to see that the man had just died. Utterson saw a small broken bottle near the body. He smelled something strong in the air and knew what it was: poison. The man had killed himself.

"We have come too late," Utterson said, "to save Dr. Jekyll or to get even with Mr. Hyde. All we can do now is look for the dead body of Dr. Jekyll."

Dr. Jekyll used only a small part of the large building for his laboratory. The building had many closets and out-of-the-way places. Poole and Utterson went over every bit of the place. But they did not find the body of poor Dr. Jekyll.

"Maybe he is under the floor," Poole said. "Hyde could have put the body under the floor."

"Or maybe he got away from Hyde," Utterson said. "I'll go look at the door."

He went over to the door—the very door that began this strange story. He looked it over with

great care. The door had not been used in a very long time. He found the key, the key that Hyde had used. It was broken into two pieces. It looked as if someone had stepped on it. The men looked at each other. You could see they didn't understand.

"This is beyond me, Poole," Utterson said. "Let us go back to the laboratory." Poole followed the lawyer. Again, they looked over Jekyll's secret room.

They walked around the dead body on the floor. The lawyer looked over the things that lay near the fire. He came to a table. You could see someone had been working with some white powder. "That is the same drug I was always bringing him," Poole said.

Utterson looked over the table that had the tea things on it. He found a book, still open. It was a holy book. At the sides of the pages, someone had been writing dirty words. Utterson gave a start. The writing was Dr. Jekyll's!

Next they came to a big standing mirror. It was turned so all you could see was the rest of the room. "That mirror has seen some strange things, sir," Poole said.

"Funny it's here," Utterson said. "What did Jekyll want with it?" Then he stopped talking. He suddenly knew he was talking as though Jekyll were dead. "What *does* Jekyll use it for?" he asked.

"I'm sure I don't know," Poole said.

Next they came to Jekyll's desk. On it was a big envelope with Mr. Utterson's name on it. The writing was in Dr. Jekyll's hand. The lawyer opened it. A few pieces of paper fell to the floor. One of them was a will—Dr. Jekyll's will. But as he read it, Utterson's eyes opened wide in surprise. It had been changed. Before, everything had gone to Mr. Hyde. Now everything went to him— G. J. Utterson. He looked at Poole, then back at the paper.

"My head is going around and around," he said to Poole. "I don't understand. Hyde was living here for eight days. He *had* to have seen this new will. It cuts him off. But he didn't burn it or throw it away. Why?"

Utterson picked up the next paper. He cried out: "Poole, look at this! It's a note from Dr. Jekyll, in his own hand. It has the date on it—today's date. That means he was alive as late as today! He must have escaped from Hyde somehow. Or maybe he has killed himself in some other place. We must be careful. Perhaps Jekyll is still alive. Then his good name is done for. That murderer Hyde has been staying here, with the police looking all over London for him."

"What does the note say, sir?" Poole asked.

"I'm almost afraid to read it," Utterson said. "But I must." He looked at the note. It said:

My dear Utterson,

By the time you read this, I will be gone. How it will come about, I cannot say. But I am sure my end is at hand. Go now, and read the letter Dr. Lanyon gave you just before he died. It is all right to read it now.

Your poor, unhappy friend,

Henry Jekyll

"Was there something else in the big envelope?" Utterson asked.

"Here it is, sir," Poole said. He gave the lawyer a bunch of papers, tied up and closed. Utterson put it in his coat pocket.

"Don't say a word about this to anyone, Poole," the lawyer said. "I'm going home now. It's ten o'clock, but I will be back before midnight. We will send for the police then. I don't know if Jekyll is dead, or if he has run away. I can't know until I have read these papers. I need time to read them."

"I will do as you say, sir," Poole said.

They went out then. They closed the outside door, and Poole went back into Dr. Jekyll's house. Utterson went home and sat by the fire. He opened the letter Dr. Lanyon had written him. Jekyll had said it was all right to read it now. After that he would read the papers he had found in Dr. Jekyll's laboratory.

9 Dr. Lanyon's Story

On January 9th, now four days ago, a letter came from my old friend Dr. Henry Jekyll. I was surprised by this. Why had he written to me? I had just seen him the night before. We had had dinner. If he had wanted to tell me something, why hadn't he said so then? However, when I read Jekyll's letter, I began to see why. This is what it said:

Dear Lanyon,

You are one of my oldest friends. Even if we do argue now and then about medical questions, we are still good friends. If you came to me and said, "Jekyll, I need your help," I would help you. I would cut off my hand to help you. Now, Lanyon, I need your help. If you can't help me, all is lost. My life, my good name—everything I have and have worked for—all gone, if you don't help me. If you think from my words that I want you to do something wrong, read my letter. Then make up your own mind.

If you were going someplace tonight, please change your plans. This is much more important. Come to my house. Poole, my butler, will be waiting for you. I have told him what to do when you get there. Go into my laboratory with him. There, you will find a big desk with a glass front. It has seven drawers. I want you to take all the papers you find in the fourth drawer from the bottom. I mean all *papers. Leave nothing. To make sure you have the right drawer, you will see some white powder, a small bottle, and a paper book. Carry the whole drawer home with you to Cavendish Square.*

This is the first part of what I ask; now for the second part. If you get this letter in time, you can go to my house and be back before midnight. I will give you until then. By midnight, all the people who work for you will be in bed asleep.

At midnight, go to your office alone. *At that time, a man will come to your door. He will say that I sent him. Let him come in. Give him the drawer you have taken from my laboratory. You will have done your job. If you do this, I will thank you for the rest of my life. Five minutes after you have given the drawer to this man, he will tell you what this is all about. Then you will know I am not crazy. My life or death is in your hands, Lanyon. Think of me as in a dark place— awful things all around me. Serve me, my dear Lanyon. Save me!*

Your friend,

H.J.

P.S.: It just came to me that the mail may be late. Therefore, you may not get this letter until tomorrow morning. Oh, God, I hope not! In that case, go to my house as I ask. Do as I have said. Then the man will come to see you in your office at midnight tomorrow. By then, it may already be too late. If the man does not come, you will know you have seen the last of Henry Jekyll.

After I read Jekyll's letter, I thought my friend had gone crazy. But until I was sure he had gone mad, what could I do? I made up my mind. I would do as he asked in his letter. I had no idea what was going on. But his words . . . the way he said he needed my help . . . I *had* to do what he asked. I got up right away and went to Jekyll's house. Just as he had said, Poole was waiting. We went into Jekyll's laboratory, and I found the big desk. It was open, and I found the drawer he had talked about.

Poole told me he knew nothing about this—just that he had received a letter from Dr. Jekyll, the same as I. The letter had told him it was all right for me to take the drawer. I tied it up, and after thanking Poole, I went home. Still in the dark about all this, I opened the drawer to see what was inside.

I saw the white powder he had talked about. It was folded up in squares of paper—not as neatly as a drugstore did them, though. Jekyll must have done it himself. There was a small bottle full of a dark red fluid. It looked almost like blood. I opened it. It had a sharp smell that made my eyes water. What it was made of, I could not say. Then I looked over the paper book he had talked about in his letter.

It was a plain copybook, the kind schoolchildren use. Inside it, I found only a lot of dates. The dates covered many years. I saw that about a year ago, the dates had stopped quite suddenly. Here and there, he wrote something next to a date. Usually it was only a word or two, like "double." He wrote this maybe once, for every fifty dates. Once, very early in the list, I came across the words: "total failure!!!"

All this made me want to know more. But it told me almost nothing. I went on looking at the papers and other things in the drawer. I found another bottle and some paper with powder in it. There was a long list of things on another piece of paper. Jekyll had been doing some medical experiment, it seemed. It looked as if his experiment had not worked.

But what was all this really about? How could these things mean life or death to Henry Jekyll? Why did he have a man pick them up? Why didn't Jekyll himself come? Why did I have to meet this man in secret? The more I thought about it, the less I knew. I began to think that perhaps Jekyll were going crazy. He had to be. Why all this, if Jekyll were right in his mind? It smelled wrong to me. I sent my servants to bed. I went to my office. I don't know why I did it, but I also took my gun.

Just as the bells rang midnight, I heard someone at my door. I opened the door and saw a small man hiding in the shadows. "Are you from Dr. Jekyll?" I asked.

He nodded his head yes. I told him to come in. He did this. But first he looked all around the dark square. It was as if someone were after him. Or maybe he didn't want to be seen. I saw a policeman coming down the street. The small man seemed afraid that the policeman might see him. He ran inside the house, with a strange light step.

Once inside my office, where the light was bright, I got a good look at him. I had my gun in my coat pocket. I kept my hand on it. Once I saw him, I was glad I had taken my gun.

He was small, as I said. His face surprised me. It was such a mixture of strength and weakness. There was something about this little man. I did not even want to be near him. I also felt my heart slow down. It was hard to catch my breath. Why this happened, I couldn't say. It seemed that just being near him made my body act strangely.

He was dressed in a way that with any other person, might make you laugh. His clothes were of the best cloth. But they were much too big for him. His pants were rolled up to keep them off the ground. His coat hung on him. It could almost make you sick to look at this man. Why should this be so? I had never seen him before. Yet, on seeing him, I hated him. Who was he? Where did he come from? How did he even know such a good man as Dr. Jekyll? All that I saw of this man would take a very long time to write down. But it only took a few seconds for me to feel this way. The little man was in a state.

"Have you got it?" he cried. "Have you got it?" He was so upset that he even put his hand on my arm. He tried to shake me.

I pushed him away. To have him put a hand on me made my blood run cold. "Come, come, sir," I said. "I don't even know your name yet. Be seated, please." To show him I meant it, I sat down, too. I took the chair behind my desk, as I do when people come to my office.

"I beg your pardon, Dr. Lanyon," he said nicely. "What you say is right. I am so upset I forgot the proper way to act. I was sent here by your friend, Dr. Henry Jekyll." He stopped talking for a second. I could see he was trying to pull himself together. "Dr. Jekyll said there was a drawer," he added.

"There it is," I said. "Over there on the floor, near my table."

He jumped over to it, then stopped. He put a hand on his heart. I could hear his teeth grind. The look on his face was awful to see. I thought for a second he was going to pass out. "Get hold of yourself, man," I said.

He turned and gave me a terrible look. Then he opened the drawer I had brought from Jekyll's house. He took one look inside and gave a cry of joy. And the next moment he had himself under control.

"Do you have a test tube?" he asked. I got up from my chair and gave him what he asked for.

He thanked me and smiled. Then he went to work. He began to mix some of the white powder with the red fluid I had seen in the drawer. As the white powder mixed with the red liquid, the color changed. The red no longer looked like blood. It was bright red now. The stuff began to fizz out

loud. Smoke began to rise from it. The color changed to dark purple. Then it turned to a watery green. All this time, the man never took his eyes off the test tube. At last he smiled and set it down. Then he turned to me and said:

"Now I must do it. Will you be wise? Will you let me take this glass in my hand and leave? Will you talk no more? Or do you *have* to know what will happen now? Think well before you answer. Because I will do what you ask. If you let me go, things will be the same for you. You won't be any richer or wiser. Unless you think that helping a poor sick man will make you richer inside.

"Or, if you *have* to know, be careful. You may not like what you find out. For what you will see, no doctor has ever seen. What you will see may even make you powerful and famous. But it may also drive you mad."

"Sir," I said, in a voice that was cool (but inside I was far from that), "you talk in circles. I have no idea what you mean. But I have come this far. I mean to see it to the end."

"Very well," said the man. "But remember, Lanyon. You are a doctor. And what doctors see in their offices, they must not talk about. It is part of being a good doctor. And now, Lanyon—you who have made fun of my ideas—watch this!"

He put the glass to his lips and drank it down. He gave an awful cry then. He almost fell down, but he grabbed the table. He held on and stood there, with his mouth open, making an awful noise. And as I looked, a change came over him. His face seemed to melt and run together. The next moment I jumped up and put my back to the wall. I raised my arm and put it in front of my eyes. I could not bring myself to watch any more of this!

"Oh, God!" I screamed, and "Oh, God!" again and again. For there before my eyes—pale and half falling down, like a man come back from the dead—there stood Henry Jekyll!

What he then told me, I cannot bring myself to write down on paper. I saw what I saw. I heard what I heard, and it made me sick at heart. I write this as I am dying. But even now, I find it hard to believe.

I can't sleep. My nights are full of fear from what I saw. I know I don't have long to live. And I will go to my death not knowing if what I saw was real. I will never get it out of my mind. And what I am about to say is the worst part.

Utterson, I must tell you the name of that evil little man. The man who came to my office that night (and Jekyll himself told me this) is known by the name of Hyde. He is wanted in every part of England as the man who killed Carew!

Hastie Lanyon

10 Henry Jekyll's Full Story of the Case

I was born in the year 18__. My family was very rich. I was healthy. People said I was handsome. I went to the best schools. I liked my schoolwork and worked very hard. People liked me, and I got along well with them. So it seemed that all would go well for me for my whole life.

But I have to say there was another side to me. I liked a good time too well. Not that this made me a bad person. But I had another picture of myself. I wanted people to think of me as a serious, hard-working man. I wanted them to see me go by and say: "There is a really good man. He doesn't waste his time. He does his work."

Because I felt this way, I did a thing I should not have done. During the day, I would be the serious Dr. Jekyll, liked by all people. But at night, I would go out and have a wild time. Anyone who saw the wild Jekyll would not believe it was the same man. This went on for years—in fact, for most of my life.

So it happened that when I reached middle age, I realized I had been leading two lives for as long as I could remember. When I began to add up what I had done in life, I saw this. It troubled me. Some men would have said, "So what?" But not I. Because I had always aimed high in life, it filled me with shame.

It was this feeling of shame that made me begin to think that I was really two people. Not that what I did when I went out at night was all that bad. But when you put it next to what I did as the good Dr. Jekyll, it seemed terrible.

Of course, almost everyone has two sides. One is good, the other evil. In me, because I lived two lives, these sides got further and further away from each other. I began to think long and hard about this. The two sides of most people aren't that far apart. Mine were.

Not that I said one thing, then did another. Each side of me was very serious about what it did. I was just as serious in my wild nights as I was in my good days. But being this way led me to study why people are the way they are.

I spent years studying this. In fact, it is this study that has brought me to such a sad end. My studies may have brought me closer to the truth than anyone has known. But oh, what it has cost me!

I know now that man is not one person, but really two. Maybe others who follow me will find out more about this. It may be that each and every person has two sides. I think I found this out because of the two lives I led. I knew I was just as much the wild Jekyll as the good one. And I knew both were real people living inside the same skin.

I began to dream of an experiment—something no one had ever tried. I would try to split my two parts. If I could do this, my life would be trouble-free. That is, the serious Dr. Jekyll would go his own way. He would be good and help the sick. He would be the best man the world had ever seen. Also, he would not lie awake each night, thinking of what his other side had done. His mind would be free to think of higher things.

As to the other Jekyll, he would go his own way. He would do all the shame-filled things he liked to do. This would mean nothing to the good Dr. Jekyll. Both sides of me would be happy. Both of us would do what we wanted. So, you see, I began my experiment in the hope that I could make the world a better place. Maybe I could make myself and all other people happy.

As I went on with my study, I learned which drugs can act upon the two sides of man. I found that far from being hard to split these two sides, it was easy—in fact, too easy. Some drugs can shake apart the pieces of man as a strong wind can blow leaves off a tree.

Now I will not go into the names of these drugs. I will not tell you how I did my experiment. This is for two reasons. First, I have found out I was wrong in my idea. I didn't make things any better by splitting my two sides. If anything, I made everything worse—worse than I can tell. Because when you split the two halves, one of them becomes worse. It becomes something so very evil that you cannot bear it.

The second reason I won't give the names of these drugs is also important. My experiment was not complete. The thing I let loose from inside me was wilder than I was. I could not control it. In fact, it began to control *me*. The worst part was this: This other thing *was* myself. It was just as real as the good Dr. Jekyll.

When I first found the drugs that could do this, I did not try them out. I was afraid. Such strong drugs could also kill. If I took just a tiny bit too much, I might die. Or worse, the drug might never let Dr. Jekyll come back. I was afraid. But I had to know if the drug would really work.

I had all the parts to my formula, but one. It was a certain salt. I sent for it from a large drug firm in London. Finally I had everything I needed. Then one night I mixed together all the parts of my formula. I sat and looked as it changed color. It fizzed and smoked. Once it cooled off, I drank it down.

I got awful pains right away. I felt that my bones would break. Then the pains began to go away. I felt as if I were coming out of a sickness— really getting well. Then I became more than

well. I felt better than I had in my whole life. I felt young and happy. The drug had made me a new man!

In my mind I felt a new freedom. I didn't care what I did. No matter what it was, it was all right with me. What did I care what others thought? They were all fools, and below me. What I did to them didn't matter. I was free of my other, good side. It made me happy. I reached out my hands with joy. That's when I discovered something. I was smaller in size!

I didn't have a mirror in my laboratory then. I had to see what I looked like. It was very late at night—almost morning. I knew Poole and all the others in the house were asleep. I made up my mind. I would go outside my laboratory in my new form. I went out into the yard. I looked up at the sky. The stars were still out. I thought to myself, "Even the stars, old as they are, have never seen anything like me!" I made my way through the yard and into the house. I went upstairs and into my bedroom. There, in the mirror, for the first time, I saw the face of Edward Hyde.

What I write now are just my ideas about Hyde. There is no way of knowing if they are really true. But I think they are probably correct. I saw that Hyde was smaller than Jekyll. I think this is because most of my life, I had been a good man. My evil side had never had the chance to grow big and strong. But Hyde also seemed to be younger than Jekyll. This was probably because he was not tired or used up the way the good side of me was. After all, as a doctor, I had worked long and hard. Hyde had never worked a day in his life.

In the same way that people could look at Dr. Jekyll and say, "This is a good man—I can tell by his face," people could look at Hyde's face and see that he was evil. Yet when I looked upon the face of Hyde, I didn't turn away. Instead, it made me happy to see that ugly face. Because that ugly thing was myself, too. He was just as much I as the good Dr. Jekyll.

There is more to it than this. Hyde seemed much more alive than Jekyll. So full of life was Hyde, he could hardly stand still. As I looked upon his face, I knew something else, too. No one could ever see Hyde's face without feeling uneasy. No one could ever like him. I think this was because when we see most people, we see both sides of them in their faces: the good and the bad mixed together. In Hyde there was none of that mixture. He was evil, through and through. How could anyone look upon him and not turn away?

I did not stand before the mirror too long. It was getting late. I had to get back to my laboratory. I still had to try the second part of my experiment. I had to see if I could turn myself back into Dr. Jekyll. I was afraid. Maybe I would have to stay Mr. Hyde forever. And I had to be careful, too. If any of my servants saw me, they would not know me. No one had ever seen Hyde back then. Poole and the others might think I was a stranger who had come to steal Dr. Jekyll's things.

I went back to my laboratory. I made the drug and drank it down. Again, I had the pains. Again, I felt sick. But in the end, I was once more Henry Jekyll.

I should have stopped the experiment right then and there. You see, when I took the drug, there was something I didn't know. I didn't know if, when I took it, the evil side or the good side of me would come out. I had hoped it would be the side that was all good. Maybe it was my own fault. If I had been thinking good thoughts when I took the drug, maybe the good side would have come out. I would have become an angel, not a devil.

But the drug played no favorites. It was as if someone were opening the door to a jail. What was inside ran out. What ran out was Hyde. Now I was split into two people: Dr. Jekyll and Mr. Hyde. But where was the good part? Hyde was all evil. But as Jekyll, I was still the same man—still part Hyde, under my skin. Where was the angel I had hoped to set free? The experiment had gone wrong. I had let loose a devil!

As I have said, even though I was getting older, the dark side of me was still there. I would still go out, once in a while, and carry on. Each time I did this, I would feel bad. I had used my time poorly. I could have been helping the sick, I thought. The two sides were tearing me apart. This was where Mr. Hyde came in.

All I had to do was take the drug. Then it wasn't Dr. Jekyll who went out to carry on at night. It was Mr. Hyde. And Hyde never lost sleep about it. He had a great time doing it. Dr. Jekyll's good name was safe. I loved the idea.

I began to make a new life for my other self. I got the house in Soho for Hyde to live in. And I furnished it. Soho was far away. Everyone knew that a good man like Dr. Jekyll would never live in Soho. It made me feel safer. I also found a woman to keep house for Hyde. I picked her because I knew she would keep her mouth shut.

Then I spoke to Poole and the others who worked for me. I told them what Mr. Hyde looked like. I said he was to have full run of my house. They were to do what Hyde told them. I even went to my own house as Hyde, so they would know me. It was then, Utterson, that I drew the will that upset you so much. I had to do it. What if something happened to Jekyll? What if he could never come back? That would mean that Hyde had no money. But Hyde *was* I. Wasn't the money just as much his as Dr. Jekyll's?

Once I had no worry about money, I felt safe. Now, many men pay others to do their dirty work. Their good names stay safe. But there was never a man like me in this world before. All my dirty work could be done by Hyde. He liked doing it! And in a way, Hyde was not a real person. How could anyone ever catch him? I could get away with anything.

By day, I was the good Dr. Jekyll. Jekyll had no fun. Jekyll had only the highest thoughts. Inside, the idea of it all made me laugh. I was like a child on the last day of school. All I had to do was go into my laboratory and take the drug. Then out would skip Hyde, ready to have his dirty fun.

Now, when Jekyll went out to have his good times, they weren't always that evil. They were just not things Jekyll would do. But the things Hyde did, well . . . they were something else again. Hyde was a monster. There was nothing too low or too evil for him.

At times, I would think back on Hyde's evil acts and shake my head. How *could* he have done those things? I was so far gone with the drug and my two lives that I was forgetting something: Hyde *was* I. I was lying to myself. I would say: 'What an awful thing to do. But after all, *I* didn't do it. It was Mr. Hyde." And it went on and on that way.

As to what things Hyde did, I won't write them down. To say they were evil is enough. But things began to catch up with me. You know how it all began. Your cousin Enfield told you about it. It started when Hyde ran the little girl down in the street.

When Enfield grabbed Hyde, I was in deep trouble. If Hyde were taken to jail, Jekyll could never come back. Hyde had to get free of Enfield. That's why he paid the money to the girl's family. But to do that, he had to use Jekyll's name. Even to get the check, Hyde had to go inside my laboratory building. And Enfield saw him do this. It was just luck that Enfield didn't know it was the back door to Jekyll's laboratory. I was afraid I would be found out.

So the next day, Dr. Jekyll put lots of money in the bank under the name of Edward Hyde. I worked out a different handwriting for Hyde, for the checks he used. It was still a lot like my own handwriting, but different enough. I felt safe.

Then two months before the Carew murder, something else happened. I had been out late the night before, as Jekyll. When I woke up, I knew I was in my own bed. I was in my own house. All my things were around me. But I felt funny. Somehow, it all looked wrong to me.

I knew I was in Jekyll's house, in Jekyll's bed. But it felt as if I were in the house in Soho, in Hyde's bed. What was going on here? I shook my head and went back to sleep. When I woke again, my hand was near my face. I looked at it and gave a start. It wasn't my hand. It was the hand of Edward Hyde!

I must have looked at the hand for a minute or so before it sank in. Suddenly, I was filled with fear—more fear than I have ever known in my life. I got out of bed and rushed to my mirror. What I saw made my blood run cold. I can't tell you how I felt at that moment. Yes, I had gone to bed as Henry Jekyll. But I had woken up as Mr. Hyde! How did it happen? And worse, what could I do about it? It was late in the morning, and Poole and the others were up and around. How could I get to my laboratory and not be seen?

I had to go down the stairs, out the door, and across the yard to my laboratory. Maybe I could cover my face. But how could I hide the fact that Hyde was so much thinner and shorter than Jekyll? Anyone who saw Hyde would know it wasn't Jekyll.

Then I smiled. It would be easy. I had been so afraid that I had forgotten one thing. All the people in my house had seen Hyde before. I could go to the laboratory as Hyde. No one would say a word.

I went downstairs and started for the laboratory. Along the way, Bradshaw saw me. The look on his face was really something to see. I knew what he was thinking. What was Mr. Hyde doing here at this hour? What must have gone through Bradshaw's mind when, ten minutes later, I came back as Dr. Jekyll! I had gotten away with it, but it had been a close call.

I was afraid. I saw the handwriting on the wall. It didn't look good. Things had taken a bad turn. I also saw something new about Hyde. He was growing bigger! As I have said, Hyde was smaller because my evil side had had no chance to grow. Now with all the time I was spending as Hyde, he was getting stronger. Would he grow bigger and stronger than Jekyll? And if he did, would Jekyll then get smaller? Or would Hyde take over everything? Would it be the end of Dr. Jekyll?

Then there was the drug I was taking. A few times, it hadn't worked. I had to take more and more each time. By now, I had to double the amount to change back to Dr. Jekyll. But that morning when I woke up as Hyde, I had taken nothing the night before. Hyde *was* taking me over! It could not go on this way.

One of us had to go. But which? To give up Hyde would mean to give up my wild nights. I would have to do things as Jekyll. I might even be seen. My good name would be lost. But to give up Jekyll was as bad. How could I live as Hyde? How could I be a man with no friends—a monster?

I made up my mind. Hyde had to go. I felt better once I had decided this. True, Jekyll would miss his good times. But he had had enough of them lately. What I hadn't thought of was how strong Hyde had become. I hadn't known he would fight being sent away.

Yes, I liked being the good Dr. Jekyll. I liked having many friends. I liked hearing people say what a nice man I was. I told myself I was rid of Hyde. But I lied to myself. I did not get rid of the house in Soho. I did not burn Hyde's clothes. They were still in my laboratory if I wanted them.

I tried hard to be Dr. Jekyll for two months. I gave dinner parties. I went to church. I began to see my old friends. I helped the sick. I worked hard, night and day. I was the best of men. I kept telling myself this was the way I should be.

But there, in my laboratory, was the drug. It called out to me in my dreams. I wanted to be free again—to do what I felt like doing at any time. I missed being Hyde. I missed the drug. Then, one night, I mixed the drug and drank it down!

I don't believe drug users or drinkers know what a chance they take. They only think of feeling good. They only think of themselves. I didn't think of the chance I was taking. Most of all, I wasn't remembering that Hyde was a monster. I took the chance, and I lost. Hyde had been shut up for two months. He had been caged so long that he came out roaring. When I took the drug, I could feel it. Hyde was stronger than ever. He would stop at nothing now.

As to the murder of Carew, what can I say? Carew was such a good man. When he had asked Hyde for directions, Hyde had seen that goodness in him. Hyde wanted to get back at all good men. Dr. Jekyll was the good man who had shut him away. But Dr. Jekyll was also Hyde. Standing there before him was Carew. This was someone he could hurt and not be hurt himself. And what he did to Carew was to kill him. To make it worse, the killing of Carew meant nothing to him. He was as a sick child who breaks a toy. And he enjoyed it!

It was as if all hell were let loose in me. I, or Hyde, began to jump up and down on the body of Carew. I was like a crazy man. I hit him again and again. I only stopped when I got tired. But when I stopped, I suddenly knew what I had done. Poor Carew was dead. And if the police were to catch Hyde, I was a dead man, too. I ran away, but I was still happy about what I had done.

I ran to my house in Soho. I burned all my papers. I had to. If the checkbook were discovered, I could be found. Yet all the time I did these things, I was happy. I even had ideas of how I could kill people. And that made me happy, too. I hurried to the laboratory and mixed the drug. I even sang a little song as I mixed it. Then I drank down the drug.

In a few minutes there stood Henry Jekyll, with tears in his eyes. Jekyll was sorry about what Hyde had done. He was crying and praying. How could I have done it, I asked? My life passed before my eyes. I thought of when I was a child, when I took walks with my father. I thought of how hard I had worked in school—of how hard I had worked as a doctor. Almost all my life, I had done good things. How could I have killed poor Carew? How could there be anything so evil inside such a good man? Again, I cried over what I had done as Hyde.

Then, suddenly, I felt better. It was over for good now. I could never be Hyde again. I could never take the drug again. My fight with myself was over. To take the drug again would mean death— for both Jekyll *and* Hyde. Never again would I mix the drug. I burned Hyde's clothes. Then I broke his key to the laboratory under my foot. I was free of Hyde forever!

The next day the papers had the news. Someone had seen the murder of Carew. All of London knew that Hyde was the killer. Hyde had not known Carew when he killed him. But Carew had been a very important man. The police would never give up looking for Hyde. It made me feel better. I knew that if Hyde showed his face he would hang for Carew's murder.

I began a new life. I spent all my time doing good deeds. I helped the sick. It was as if a bad dream had come to an end. I would be a new man—a better man—even better than Jekyll had ever been. But I didn't know my dark side well enough. It seemed the more good I did, the more I wanted to go out and carry on. I knew I couldn't carry on as Hyde. He was wanted for murder. It was as Jekyll that I would go out. And so I did.

There comes an end to all things. And this time when I went out as Jekyll, I also came to an end. I had thought it would be like going back to the old days—the days before I began taking the drug. It was a fine, clear January day. There was a little melted snow under my feet as I walked down the street. In the park, birds sang. Even though it was January, I could smell a bit of spring in the air.

I sat in the sun on a park bench. It was warm there. I looked at the people going by. I would see one man and think: "I am as good a man as he. I am happy to be such a good man." Suddenly, I felt strange. I began to shake. I felt as if I were getting sick. Then it all passed.

I began to feel better. Better? I never felt better in my life. I looked at the people passing. The same people now looked different to me. Who cared about them? They were below me. They were nothing. That's when I looked down and saw my hand—no, not my hand. It was the hand of Edward Hyde!

A minute ago, I had been the best of men. I had had all a man could ever want. Now I was the killer of Carew. I was wanted by the police. Every hand in London would be raised against me.

I nearly lost my head at first. Maybe Jekyll would have given up. But Hyde had always had a fast mind. In the past he had gotten himself out of some bad spots by fast thinking. So he would this time. The drug that would turn me back into Jekyll was in my laboratory. But I had broken the key. How could I get the drug? I couldn't just go to my laboratory. If my servants saw Hyde, it meant the end for me. I needed someone to help me. That's when I thought of Lanyon.

But how could I get to Lanyon? Even if I could stay away from the police, it was going to be hard. How could I get Lanyon to enter my laboratory and get the drug for me? My good man, Poole, would never let someone else inside my laboratory. Then I had an idea. My handwriting was the same, even when I was Hyde. It was just a little different when I wrote Hyde's checks.

I got a passing cab. The driver looked at my clothes. They didn't fit me. He thought I looked funny and smiled. Hyde gave him a look of such evil that he stopped smiling right away. It was a good thing, too. Hyde would have hurt him. The cab took me to a hotel in Portland Street. Hyde used the same look on the man at the hotel desk. Afraid of Hyde, he got me a room quickly. He also gave me a pen and some paper.

It was a strange thing about Hyde. Here he was on the run. But through it all, he was the same Hyde. He was cool and calm. Oh, he was still full of evil thoughts. He still wanted to hurt others. He would have laughed while he did it, too. Yet, he was still able to write two letters. The letters were to Lanyon and Poole. He told Poole what to do. He asked Lanyon for help.

He spent the rest of the day in the hotel room, biting his nails. He ate a meal, sitting alone with his fears. When it got dark, he went out and got a cab. He didn't make the cab driver take him to Lanyon's house. He had him drive all around London. He didn't want anyone to know where he was going. After a time he had the driver stop. He walked the rest of the way to Lanyon's. He was taking a chance doing this. He knew he looked funny in clothes that didn't fit. This would draw people's eyes to him. And Hyde was a wanted man.

He walked fast, talking to himself as he went. He stayed in the shadows. Once a woman came up to talk to him. I think she was selling matches. He hit her in the face, and she ran away. At last, he got to Lanyon's house.

At Lanyon's, I mixed the drug and again became Dr. Jekyll. I saw what this did to Lanyon. Poor Lanyon couldn't live with what he saw. I saw the look of horror on his face. But the horror Lanyon felt was nothing, next to what I felt. There was a chance I might stay Hyde forever. It was far worse than the chance that I might hang for the murder of Carew.

I made my way home. I don't know how. It was
like a bad dream. I fell into my bed and slept like a
dead man. No dream woke me. Nothing could. I
woke up after a day's sleep, feeling better. Yes, I
knew that Hyde was still inside me. I knew he
would try to get out again. But I was home. I was

in my own house, and safe. I could now get to my laboratory and the drugs, if Hyde took over again.

So it began. I never knew when Hyde would come back. I spent almost all my time taking the drug. I kept trying to stay Dr. Jekyll. It was like a war. And I was losing it. I never knew when the pains and sick feeling would come over me. If I went to sleep, even for a nap, I would wake up as Hyde. It was like a bad dream that I couldn't wake up from.

Jekyll grew weak from no sleep and from using the drug so much. But Hyde was getting stronger all the time. Jekyll was sick. Hyde was well. Hyde was full of hate. He wanted to go out and kill people. But he knew if the police saw him, he would hang. It made him madder. Now the pains when I turned into Hyde weren't so great. It was getting easier to be Hyde than to stay Jekyll. The only thing that kept me going was the hate I had for Hyde. I had to stay alive. I couldn't let Hyde loose on the world.

And Hyde hated me, too. It made him crazy when I took the drug. It was like killing himself when I did. Yet he knew I had to take the drug. If I didn't take it, Hyde would hang. It drove him wild. He began to pull little tricks on Jekyll.

I had a holy book I was reading. It helped me to fight Hyde. I would wake up as Jekyll and find dirty words written all over the pages. He burned my letters. He burned the picture of my father. He would have killed Jekyll, if he could. *But that would also kill him.* He would scream aloud, he was so angry. In a way, I could almost feel sorry for him.

Now I feel my life slipping away. I can't fight Hyde any longer. Just to write this down is using me up. Any second, he will take over. If I get too weak, he will come back. But I have to tell the whole story.

This evil dream might go on forever. I might have to spend the rest of my life fighting Hyde. I might spend my years as part man, part monster. Could hell itself be worse than this? I am paying for what I did—both as Hyde and as Jekyll. And now, the worst has happened. I am running out of the drug!

I sent Poole to the biggest drugstore in London. I wrote down what I needed. He came back, and I tried it. It didn't work at all this time. It changed color and fizzed. But the changes were a bit off. The colors were, too. At first, I thought that Hyde was getting stronger than the drug. But I see now that the drug was not pure enough.

I sent Poole all over London. I had to get some of the old drug, or Hyde would win. I got some at last. I also know what was wrong. It wasn't that the new drug wasn't pure. It was that the *old* drug hadn't been pure. There was something in it that hadn't belonged there. But it was that *something* that had made it work. And I don't, for the life of me, know what that was.

About a week has gone by since I began to write this. I am writing this as Jekyll, for the last time. I ran out of the old drug today. Once I fall asleep, or once it wears off, I will become Hyde forever. This will be the last time I can look at myself in the mirror and see Jekyll. True, the Jekyll I see is a spent man. He is pale and thin. He looks like a man about to die. In a way, I am about to die.

I must hurry and write this down. I don't know when the drug will wear off. I also have to be careful. If Hyde finds this story, he will tear it up. But I know something about Hyde. He is feeling weak, too.

About half an hour from now, when I am Hyde again, what will happen? Will the police find Hyde? Will he hang for the murder of Carew? Or will he be strong enough to kill himself before the police find him? I hope so. But I can't say for sure. What I do know is this: This is my true hour of death. Anything that happens after this happens to someone else. It happens to Hyde.

So I lay down my pen. I have told it all. I will seal it up in an envelope. Here then, I bring the life of that unhappy Henry Jekyll to an end.